Lisa,
May this next
healing, extra l

You have a gift that the world
is ready to receive. Give it out loudly!

Inhale the opportunity.
Exhale the doubt.

R. L. S

I am ready. I am loved.
I am exactly where I'm meant to be.

the words I read to
{You}

Cover design: Jenny Pugh
Front cover photographer: Sandra Johnson
Yoga model in pictures: Jami Johnson
Back cover photographer: Thu Tran
Editor: Bryonie Wise

First Printing: 2016

www.wildleafyoga.com

Dedication

To the ones who read between the lines.
To the ones who crave words for their soul.
To all the wild ones.

Preface

I am thankful to personally know a few of the writers and I am honored to share each and every word of their wisdom.

I hope you find a piece of your heart through these readings.

I hope you dig deep and follow these authors because they are truly incredible.

I created this book because of the inspiration and empowerment these readings gave me during my bright, sun shining days and the dark, cold lonely nights.

After my heart cried out with either happiness or sadness, I knew I needed to put the words I had discovered in my moments of truth into the universe.

I have made it part of my personal and teaching practices to always begin with a mantra or affirmation and end with a soulful, heart pulling, word-gasm reading.

The universe spoke back to me and I realized that people loved the affirmations and readings just as much as I do.

I spent countless hours emailing, typing, blogging and texting nightly readings to my students.

I finally realized that I was being called to do something bigger—I needed to make a book of the words I read.

The words that we may never get the chance to read because we didn't know the book existed.

These are small passages—a tiny fraction—of beauty from amazing writers.

***

Feel the beat in your belly and the rhythm of your heart.

Inhale the opportunity.
Exhale the doubt.

You were meant to be here.

R. L. Livingston

There is no right way to get to where you're going. The joy in the journey comes from the beautiful space that we hold in between.

R. L. Livingston

Journey Home

You have forgotten your purpose.
You have buried your soul.
You have locked up your truth.

You have been swallowed by rules, expectations and perceptions of thousands of other view points.

On your journey to coming home to yourself, you will step off the yellow brick road.

You will get turned around on the road less traveled.

You will hop many more fences looking for greener grass on the other side.

Amidst this journey to coming home to yourself, I suggest you honor the unexpected turns, the bumps in the road, and the grass that was never greener on the other side.

Continue to move forward.

Smile and take a deep breath.

You will soon realize that the journey to coming home to yourself will be the foundation of your new home.

When you arrive, you will remember who you are instead of who you thought you should be.

R. L. Livingston

Something beautiful happens on the mat for the student who stays with yoga practice even for a short time.

An awareness begins to dawn.

Having been immersed in an outwardly focused culture, most of us come to yoga in search of something we do not have, something we cannot even name.

As the weeks turn into months, though, we begin to understand that we are no longer seeking something outside ourselves, or something we do not have.

A powerful understanding starts to take shape.

Our attention shifts from what we can get to who we can be.

Without anyone needing to tell us—but simply by spending time on the mat with ourselves.

We arrive at the conclusion that we are the ones we have been waiting for.

Rolf Gates

Honor the Beginning

Beginnings can be delicate or explosive.

They can start almost invisibly or arrive with a big bang.

Beginnings hold the promise of new lessons to be learned, new territory to be explored and old lessons to be recalled, practiced, and appreciated.

Beginnings hold ambiguity, promise, fear, and hope.

Let yourself begin anew.

Pack your bags.

Choose carefully what you bring, because packing is an important ritual.

Take along some humility and the lessons of the past.

Toss in some curiosity and excitement about what you haven't yet learned.

Say your goodbyes to those you're leaving behind.
Don't worry who you will meet or where you will go.

The way has been prepared.
The people you are to meet will be expecting you.

A new journey has begun.

Let it be magical.
Let it unfold.

Melody Beattie

Through the storm, the sunflower's scattered seeds grew wild and tall.

Full of light and color.

Demonstrating the ability to grow through the toughest kind of weather.

The kind that breaks you down to your soil, disrupts your newborn roots, pushes you to a new place where you can finally grow.

And demonstrating patience—it may take time to grow, but no one can refute that gloriously radiant and vibrant bloom.

Hannah Hutcheson

I wish for you:

Comfort on difficult days, smiles when sadness intrudes
rainbows to follow the clouds, laughter to feel your lips,
sunsets to warm your heart, gentle hugs when spirits sag,
friendship to brighten your day, beauty for your eyes to see,
confidence for when you doubt, faith so that you can believe,
courage to know yourself, patience to accept the truth, and
Love to complete your life.

Ralph Waldo Emerson

Gratitude unlocks the fullness of life.

It turns what we have into enough and more.

It turns denial into acceptance,
Chaos to order, confusion to clarity.

It can turn a meal into a feast,
A house into a home,
A stranger into a friend.

Gratitude makes sense of our past,
Brings peace for today,
And creates a vision for tomorrow.

Meoldy Beattie

Each time we come to the mat, we have an opportunity to work the entire path, moment by moment.

As we move through the postures we are constantly enacting each aspect of the path.

Our bodies, our breath, our minds, and our choices are being refined in the laboratory that is our yoga mat.

As this symphony becomes established on our mats, it becomes established in our lives as well.

Driving to work, mailing a letter, meeting a friend for lunch, all become part of the uninterrupted flow of our yoga practice.

We are doing our yoga all the time.

Rolf Gates

There's Magic in the Unknown

Sometimes we're out of ideas.

We think and think but nothing comes.
We don't know what's next.

It feels like we're at a dead end.

But we're not.

That void, that dreaded blank spot is a really glorious
magical place.

Sometimes we have to run out of our ideas before we can
open up to any new ones.

The reason why we can't see any further is because our ideas
are limited by the past, by past experiences, by what life has
been like before.

Our future doesn't have to be limited by our past.

Life knows that. Now we can learn it too.

We're not at a dead end.

We've reached a new beginning.

Melody Beattie

Inhale. Exhale.

Take a moment to listen to your mind and body.

*Take time to listen closely to the whispers
and the quiet screams of your soul.*

*When we explore our breath, we find that moment,
when we take the time—we discover our own cure
to our own insanity.*

R.L. Livingston

Stand tall.

Stand proud.

You've made it this far.

Smile to those who didn't think you could.

Hug the ones who knew you would.

Let go of the hands that hold you back.

Reach for the hands that lift you up.

Go your own way and discover your truth.

Make a path and get lost in your own journey.

Honor your past, respect the present, and be humble to your future.

R. L. Livingston

When we bring our attention to our breath, we are changing planes, moving from one level of existence to another.

Our suffering is largely due to our imagined relationship to the past or to the future; the breath, however, is a doorway to the present.

Not only are we gaining significant and well-documented health benefits by paying attention to our breathing, we are also consciously leaving an imagined world and entering the real.

It's powerful.

It's real.

It is the opportunity you've been waiting for.

Rolf Gates

Your life is a sacred journey.

It is about change, growth, discovery, movement, transformation; continuously expanding your vision of what is possible, stretching your soul, learning to see clearly and deeply, listening to your intuition, taking courageous challenges at every step along the way.

You are on the path ... exactly where you are meant to be right now ... And from here, you can only go forward, shaping your life story into a magnificent tale of triumph, of healing, of courage, of beauty, of wisdom, of power, of dignity, and of love.

Caroline Adams

Coming home to ourselves is stopping outwardly, and consciously redirecting our attention inwards in order to engage and know the ceaseless stream of our inner experience as it now occurs.

It is directing our attention to become aware of the sensations in our body, feelings within our chest, stomach, and belly, and the thoughts occupying our present moment.

Coming home to ourselves reflects taking a personal interest in ourselves, as if we too mattered.

Michael Nagel

Honor the days, the ones where the falls cause bruises and wounds, and the anger precedes reaction.

By taking a moment on those days, we listen to our bodies, slow our minds and fall in love with the process.

R.L. Livingston

Yoga wears away the self-centered fear.

Each posture, each breath we take, loosens our grip on the life we have lived and allows for the birth of a new one.

Eventually, caught up in the beautiful work of being present for grace, we forget about ourselves, and through self-forgetting we find ourselves.

Rolf Gates

You fall with grace and stand with beauty.

R. L. Livingston

Fierce with Grace

The dark places I so desperately search for a light in can be navigated with patience, breath and heart—even with eyes closed, I can feel around for the thing I thought I lost and realize it will always be in the last place I put it down.

All along, in the search for a new home and here it was, inside of me the whole time.

Bryonie Wise

All the Hemispheres

Leave the familiar for a while.
Let your senses and bodies stretch out

Like a welcomed season
Onto the meadows and shores and hills.

Open up to the Roof.
Make a new water-mark on your excitement
And love.

Like a blooming night flower,
Bestow your vital fragrance of happiness and giving
Upon our intimate assembly.

Change rooms in your mind for a day.

All the hemispheres in existence
Lie beside an equator
In your heart.

Greet Yourself
In your thousand other forms
As you mount the hidden tide and travel
Back home.

All the hemispheres in heaven
Are sitting around a fire
Chatting

While stitching themselves together
Into the Great Circle inside of
You.

Hafiz

Most of us come to the mat with a mind that is out of control and a poor nonexistent relationship to our bodies.

Nonetheless, we stay with it.

We find that amidst the jumble of pride, desire, aversion and fear, there is a still point, a part of ourselves bearing witness to it all that wants to come back to the next yoga class.

Amidst the din of our resistance to life, the clamor of our fears, there is a quiet voice whose guidance we learn to listen to and to trust.

In the mirror of our yoga postures we begin to see that we are not our pride, our fear, our desire.

Over time we find that we are not many other things as well.

We make a begining, we develop a love and respect for the person we meet in the mirror of our yoga practice.

We find that we would rather be ourselves, imperfectly, than someone else perfectly.

Rolf Gates

Walk Slowly

It only takes a reminder to breathe, a moment to be still,
and just like that, something in you settles, softens, makes
space for imperfection.

The harsh voice of judgment drops to a whisper and you
remember again that life isn't a relay race; that waking up
to life is what we were born for.

As many times as you forget, catch yourself charging
forward, that many times you can make the choice
to stop, to breathe, to be, and to walk slowly into the
mystery.

Danna Faulds

Honoring our own voices and choices is not easy in a world that presents us with more voices and choices than ever.

To do so, we must resist the tide that would pull us along with the crowd. And to do that, we must learn to celebrate who we are.

While life provides us with mentors and role models to guide us along the way, in the end we must depart from all mentors and models.

Their path may not be our path, and their final destination may not be our own.

The sages say that our job is not to become our teachers, parents, friends, or advisors, but to become ourselves.

Often the hardest part of that equation is learning to trust the process, savor the moments, and fall back in love with who we are.

Patricia Spadaro

For what it's worth: it's never too late or, in my case, too early to be whoever you want to be.

There's no time limit, stop whenever you want.

You can change or stay the same, there are no rules to this thing.

We can make the best or the worst of it.

I hope you make the best of it.
And I hope you see things that startle you.
I hope you feel things you never felt before.
I hope you meet people with a different point of view.

I hope you live a life you're proud of.

If you find that you're not, I hope you have the courage to start all over again.

Eric Roth

There is a sun to your moon.

A soul to your body.

A yes to your no.

You are alive while you are dying.

Sleeping while you are awake.

There is a dream to your nightmare.

A forever to your end.

A friend to your stranger.

A movement to your stillness.

A hello to your goodbye.

A yesterday to your today.

A past to your present.

A wholeness to your emptiness.

A love to your hatred.

A something to your nothing.

But most of all, there is a happiness to your sadness.

And if you ever lose it, just remember, soon enough it will find you and the ride back will be the most precious thing known to your earth.

r.m.drake

Awaken to the Storyteller Within

Each of us has a story to tell and our own way of sharing it with the world. It comes out through our words, through our work, and through the simple actions of our daily life.

Listen to the stories of the people around you.
Listen with your soul.

Learn to value with out judging and listen with
an open heart to the beauty of each story and
the importance of the storyteller.

Learn to value and appreciate the story you
are living now.

Awaken to the storyteller within and share your story with the world.

Tell it with joy and flair.

Commit to telling it with love and passion.

Tell it through living your life fully, doing your work well, and creating the best life you can.

Be who you are and love being that.

Melody Beattie

Truly the best way to get out of the dark is to sit in the dark.

No light. No friend. Just you—in the dark.

Once you have sat with yourself in the dark, you will discover a light is within reach, a friend is nearby, and you, yourself, are all you ever needed.

R.L. Livingston

Paradox of Our Age

The paradox of our time in history is that we have taller buildings but shorter tempers, wider Freeways, but narrower viewpoints.

We spend more, but have less, we buy more, but enjoy less. We have bigger houses and smaller families, more conveniences, but less time.

We have more degrees but less sense, more knowledge, but less judgment, more experts, yet more problems, more medicine, but less wellness.

We've learned how to make a living, but not a life. We've added years to life not life to years.

We've been all the way to the moon and back, but have trouble crossing the street to meet a new neighbor.

We conquered outer space but not inner space. We've done larger things, but not better things.

We've cleaned up the air, but polluted the soul. We've conquered the atom, but not our prejudice. We write more, but learn less. We plan more, but accomplish less. We've learned to rush, but not to wait.

Remember, to spend some time with your loved ones, because they are not going to be around forever. Remember, to say, "I love you" to your loved ones and mean it. but most of all—slow down.

Bob Moorehead

53

We must learn to trust that if we fall out of a balancing posture, rest during a vigorous class, or take a day off when we are tired, we will not lose our own respect or affection.

Many of us expect more of ourselves than we would ever ask of anyone else.

We simply cannot live up to our potential unless we are willing to live boldly, and take adaptive risks.

But if we are to continue to learn and grow, we must also know that at the end of the day there will be a home to return to, where we will be loved for our hearts as well as our deeds.

We must be steadfast in our love and respect for ourselves, both when we soar and when we stumble.

Rolf Gates

Just For Now

Just for now, without asking how, let yourself sink
into stillness.

Just for now, lay down the weight you so patiently bear upon
your shoulders.

Feel the earth receive you, and the infinite expanse of sky
grow even wider as your awareness reaches up to meet it.

Just for now, allow a wave of breath to enliven
your experience.

Breathe out whatever blocks you from the truth.

Just for now, be boundless, free, awakened energy tingling in
your hands and feet.

Drink in the possibility of being who and what you really are
so fully alive that when you open your eyes the world looks
different, newly born and vibrant, just for now.

Danna Faulds

Learn to Live with Ambiguity

Sometimes, the picture isn't finished yet.

Ideas, possibilities, hopes, dreams float around, circling us like asteroids around a planet.

These little pieces float by.

We reach for them, try to grab them in our hands, so we can connect them, force them into a whole, force them into a picture we can see, something that makes sense.

Let the pieces be.
Let yourself be.
Let life be.

Sometimes, chaos needs to precede order.

You dont have to force the pieces to fit together if it's not time.

You don't have to know.
There is power sometimes in not knowing.
There is power in letting go.

Power in waiting.
Power in stillness.
Power in trust.

There is power in letting the disconnected pieces be until they settle into a whole.

Let the pieces be, and they'll take shape.

Soon you'll see the whole picture.

Melody Beattie

Wild Geese

"You do not have to be good.

You do not have to walk on your knees
For a hundred miles through the desert, repenting.

You only have to let the soft animal of your body
love what it loves."

***

You are perfect in your wholeness.

Your wholeness includes your scars, your weaknesses, your mood swings, the days of your life you'd rather pull the covers up over your head and stay in bed.

Yoga is a practice of peeling away labels of 'good' and 'bad' and embracing whatever form of beauty you bring to your mat each day.

Poem by Mary Oliver/Writing by Liz Huntly

Breaking Surface

Let no one keep you from your journey,
no rabbi or priest, no mother
who wants you to dig for treasures
she misplaced, no father
who won't let one life be enough,
no lover who measures their worth
by what you might give up,
no voice that tells you in the night
it can't be done.

Let nothing dissuade you
from seeing what you see
or feeling the winds that make you
want to dance alone
or go where no one
has yet to go.

You are the only explorer.
Your heart, the unreadable compass.
Your soul, the shore of a promise
too great to be ignored.

Mark Nepo

The Lessons are Love

Courage. Faith. Patience.

Loving ourselves when it looks and feel like nobody
else cares.

Starting over again one more time, when we think
we've already started over again more times than we
should have had to.

Forgiveness. Compassion. Gentleness. Joy.

Each one is a lesson of love.

Feel your feelings.

Struggle through your situations and experiences
and emotions.

The struggle to learn isn't incidental to your purpose.

It's an integral part of your purpose, your destiny, your
reason for being.

Go through your moments of darkness and confusion,
and trust that the light will come.

Through it all, rest in one thought—you're on track.

You're on your path.

You're exactly where you were meant to be.

Melody Beattie

The Fragile Vial

"Be a spot of ground where nothing is growing,
where something might be planted,
a seed, possibly, from the Absolute."

***

Yoga shows us the temporality of everything.

We watch as our bodies change—the day-to-day fluctuations;
the steady transformation over the years as we get stronger,
as we get older.

We learn to accept that nothing is permanent, that each
practice will be different.

We learn to let go of preconceived ideas of what we can
or cannot do.

We welcome every possibility.

Poem by Rumi / writing by Liz Huntly

The pieces crumble: scattered, bent, broken.

Yet, you end up putting the crumbled, scattered, bent and broken pieces back together.

You are enlightened.

Your new masterpiece is better than the original.

R. L. Livingston

Patience is a beautiful thing.

A miraculous thing.

Find it, and maybe tomorrow you will be someone else.

That alone is everything worth waiting for.

The hurry and the wait to become more than that of what you are.

r.m. drake

Unfinished Projects

Whether your project is sewing a dress, reading a book, writing a book, building a home, or learning a lesson on your journey, learn to live comfortably with unfinished work.

Whatever you're working on, whatever you're in the midst of doesn't need to be finished, in perfect order, with all the loose ends in place for you to be happy.

Enjoy all the stages of the process you're in.

The first moments when the germ of the idea finds you.

The time before you begin, when the seed lies dormant in the ground, getting ready to grow.

The begining, and all the days through out the middle.

Those bleak days, when it looks like you're stuck and won't break through.

Those exciting days, when the project, the lesson, the life you're building takes shape and form.

Melody Beattie

There is an inner light that comes into the faces of those who have begun to walk the path. Initially, we are filled with self-conscious fear.

Our postures are all about trying to get it right. We are practicing yoga with the same suppressed hopelessness with which we experience a life that doesn' quite work.

Then, one bright morning or some dark evening, the energy begins to move.

We wake from a spiritual winter.

Oftentimes we are the last to see the difference.

Those around us are captivated by the new sparkle in our eyes, a radiance that seems to shine from within, the bloom of health.

Eventually we get it.

Slowly we awaken to these barely perceptible changes, the outer manifestations of the profound shift that is taking place in our lives.

Rolf Gates

Desiderata

"You are a child of the universe, no less than the trees and the stars; you have a right to be here.

And whether or not it is clear to you, no doubt the universe is unfolding as it should."

***

Endeavor, in your practice (and your life), to do what you feel is best, or to follow the sound advice of others.

And know, still, that you will make mistakes and that good fortune will not always appear to be on your side.

An injury, a pose that is eternally frustrating, an experience with a teacher that irritates you, are lessons that become threads in the strong weave of your practice.

In yoga (in life), we do our best to stay the course, but we also trust the wind to carry us home.

Poem by Max Ehrmann / Writing by Liz Huntly

Anything that annoys you is teaching you patience.

Anyone who abandons you is teaching you how to stand up on your own two feet.

Anything that angers you is teaching you forgiveness and compassion.

Anything that has power over you is teaching you how to take your power back.

Anything you hate is teaching you unconditional love.

Anything you fear is teaching you courage to overcome your fear.

Anything you can't control is teaching you how to let go and trust the Universe.

Jackson Kiddard

Your Body, Mind and Soul are One

Find that place of balance in nurturing all parts
of you.

Then life will begin to be magical and you'll see what you
believe.

Your feelings won't be a bother. They'll fuel your life;
they'll be the passion that adds color and zest
to your life.

Your body will lead you instinctively into what you want
and away from what you dislike.

And the longer you travel the journey to the heart, the
more you'll discover and trust your own soul.

Melody Beattie

Life is amazing.

And then it's awful.

And then it's amazing again.

And in between the amazing and awful it's ordinary
and mundane and routine.

Breathe in the amazing, hold on through the awful, and
relax and exhale during the ordinary.

That's just living heartbreaking, soul-healing, amazing,
awful, ordinary life.

And it's breathtakingly beautiful.

L.R. Knost

There is a universe outside your door, waiting to touch you, soothe you, heal you.

There is an entire world out there waiting to help you open your heart and nurture your soul.

The universe wants to teach you things, show you things, help you come more alive than you've ever been before.

Let the universe bring you all the healing you need.

Let the universe bring you alive.

Awaken to the world around you and you will awaken to yourself.

Melody Beattie

We all make choices that we have to live with.

It's not the past that kills us, it's the present moment of knowing we continue to do nothing to change the future.

R. L. Livingston

Do not let your fire go out, spark by irreplaceable spark in the hopeless swamps of the not-quite, the not-yet, and the not-at-all.

Do not let the hero in your soul perish in lonely frustration for the life you deserved and have never been able to reach.

The world you desire can be won.

It exists ... it is real ... it is possible ... it's yours.

Ayn Rand

Let Yourself Be Who You Are

It's difficult to be around people who are trying to be perfect
—perfectly healthy, perfectly polite, perfectly poised,
perfectly controlled.

Remember that being human means being imperfect, being
flawed.

Let yourself be.
Let others be.

Slouch in your chair.
Eat with the wrong fork.
Laugh out loud.

Stand up and reveal who you are and know that you're good
enough.

Stop worrying that people will find out who
you really are.

Instead, hope that they do.

Help them by openly sharing yourself and being not who
you think you should be, but who you really are.

Melody Beattie

Kindness

"Before you know what kindness really is
you must lose things,
feel the future dissolve in a moment
like salt in a weakened broth.

What you held in your hand,
what you counted and carefully saved,
all this must go so you know
how desolate the landscape can be
between the regions of kindness."

***

Yoga is a practice of non-violence, of love.

We start by learning kindness towards ourselves.

We learn to take all our sorrows and our hurt and wrap
them in the blanket of our own self-love.

And then we learn to be compassionate, we take that
blanket of love and drape it across the world.

Poem by Naomi Shihab Nye/Writing by Liz Huntly

I feel alive today because today is a blessing.

In this moment, I can find misery or meaning, boredom or motivation.

I can expand the hatred in the world, or I can amplify love.

In all the chaos, I can find stillness and joy within.

All is well, and nothing has to happen to "give" me more happiness in life.

I simply choose to be happy now, to be grateful now, to be a source of love and light for others.

I am whole.

I am ready.

This is my day.

Brendon Burchard

I have come to accept the feeling of not knowing where I am going.

And I have trained myself to love it.

Because it is only when we are suspended in mid-air with no landing in sight, that we force our wings to unravel and alas begin our flight.

And as we fly, we still may not know where we are going.

But the miracle is in the unfolding of the wings.

You may not know where you're going, but you know that so long as you spread your wings, the winds will carry you.

C. JoyBell C.

I am not perfect.
I lose my own breath.
I forget to love myself first.
I am sore after a yoga class.
I fumble my words.
I don't have all of the answers.
I curse.
I get angry.
I ignore my mind and body some days.
I cry after I fall.
I doubt my purpose.
I have bad days.
I am not less of a yogi.
I am human.

R.L. Livingston

On the Other Side of Fear is Joy

Fear can be like a brick wall on our path.

We may say we want to move forward—we want to feel
better, do something new, live differently, go to the next
place on our journey—but if we have unrecognized fears
about that, we may feel like we've hit a wall.

We don't know we're afraid, the fear is tucked and hidden
away.

All we can see is that, for some unknown reason, we can't
seem to move forward in our own life.

We're in the dark.

Gently face your fears one at a time as they arise.

Let each fear surface into consciousness.

Tell yourself you know it's there.

Then release it's energy; let it dissipate into the air.

Don't be afraid of what you'll find; the feeling is
 only fear.

All you have to do is simply face and feel your fear.

Melody Beattie

Trust the universe when the skies fall.

When the rain doesn't stop.
When the clouds won't clear.

Even when the world seems empty.

Trust the universe.

It will bring you to the place
where you're meant to be.

R.L. Livingston

Acknowledgments

My biggest thank you to my husband Ryan. You have been my biggest supporter (and yes, you are officially married to a published author).

Thank you Jami—for holding my hand through the darker days and for being my light—your photos radiate throughout this book and I thank you for bringing life to my words.

Thank you Lane Gormley—I found you when I was in search of a therapist and a grip on life yet you have given me more than what any co-pay could ever give a wandering soul.

Thank you Be Yoga and Roswell Yoga Life for creating a space for me to find my voice as a teacher and student.

Thank you Rachel for always reading after savasana—you inspired me to do the same.

Thank you Lauren for giving me "Meditations from the Mat" by Rolf Gates. You inspired my practice and teaching journey.

Thank you Bryonie Wise for taking me under your beautiful, soaring wings—your guidance truly made this book possible.

Most of all, thank you to all of my students—if you hadn't spoken and asked for a copy of the readings I share after class, this compilation of words wouldn't be nestled into your hands.

References

Adams, Caroline
www.carolinejoyadams.com
Page: 25

Beattie, Melody
Journey to the Heart
[Daily Meditations on the Path of Freeing Your Soul]
HarperSanFrancisco, 1996
www.melodybeattie.com
Pages: 7, 13, 17, 49, 59, 65, 73, 81, 85, 91, 101

Burchard, Brendon
www.brendon.com
Page: 95

C. JoyBell C.
www.cjoybellc.com
Page: 97

Drake, Robert M.
www.rmdrk.bigcartel.com
Pages: 47, 71

Ehrmann, Max
*Desiderata (*and excerpt by Liz Huntly)
The Poems of Max Ehrmann
Bruce Humphries Publishing Compan of Boston, 1948
Page: 77

Emerson, Ralph Waldo
Pages: 11

Faulds, Danna
Go In and In: Poems from the Heart of Yoga
Peaceable Kingdom Books, 2002
Pages: 41, 57

Gates, Rolf
Meditations from the Mat: Daily Reflections on the Path of Yoga
Anchor, 2002
www.rolfgates.com
Pages: 5, 15, 23, 31, 39, 55, 75

Hafiz
All the Hemispheres
Page: 37

Huntly, Liz
www.lizandroland.com
Pages: 61, 67, 77, 93

Hutcheson, Hannah
www.JustAWomanOnAJourney.com
Page: 9

Kiddard, Jackson
Anything that Annoys You
Page: 79

Knost, L. R.
Life is Amazing
www.littleheartsbooks.com
Page: 83

Moorehead, Bob
Paradox of our Age
Full essay essay appeared in 'Words Aptly Spoken,'
Dr. Moorehead's 1995 Collection of Prayers, Homilies & Monologues
Page: 53

Nagel, Michael
Coming Home to Ourselves
www.personal-authenticity-project.com/coming-home
Page: 27

Nepo, Mark
www.marknepo.com
Page: 63

Nye, Naomi Shihab
*Kindness, 1952 (*and excerpt by Liz Huntly)
Full poem: https://www.poets.org/poetsorg/poem/kindness
Page: 93

Oliver, Mary
Wild Geese (and excerpt by Liz Huntly)
Full poem: www.maryoliver.beacon.org
Page: 61

Rand, Ayn
Do Not Let Your Fire Go Out
Atlas Shrugged
www.aynrand.org
Page: 89

Roth, Eric
For What it's Worth
The Curious Case of Benjamin Button, 2008
Pages: 45

Rumi
The Fragile Vial
Page: 67

Spadaro, Patricia
Honor Yourself: The Inner Art of Giving and Receiving
Three Wings Press
Pages: 43

Wise, Bryonie
Fierce with Grace (excerpt from elephantjournal.com)
www.bryoniewise.com
Page: 35

CPSIA information can be obtained
at www.ICGtesting.com
Printed in the USA
FFOW04n1858211216
30604FF